THE IMPRESSIONISTS' RIVER

VIEWS OF THE SEINE

CLAUDE MONET'S *SUNDAY AT ARGENTEUIL*, 1872

THE IMPRESSIONISTS' RIVER

VIEWS OF THE SEINE

Universe

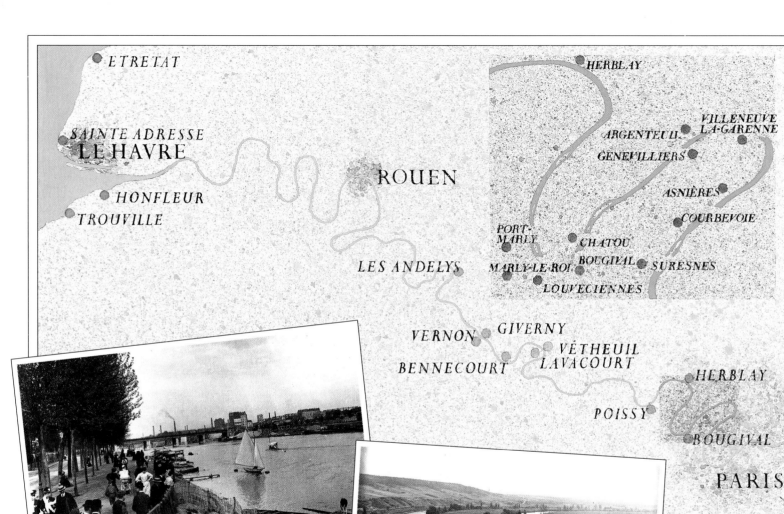

ETRETAT

SAINTE ADRESSE
LE HAVRE

HONFLEUR

TROUVILLE

ROUEN

LES ANDELYS

HERBLAY

VILLENEUVE
LA-GARENNE

ARGENTEUIL

GENEVILLIERS

ASNIÈRES

COURBEVOIE

PORT-
MARLY

CHATOU

BOUGIVAL

SURESNES

MARLY-LE-ROI

LOUVECIENNES

VERNON
GIVERNY

VÉTHEUIL
LAVACOURT

BENNECOURT

HERBLAY

POISSY

BOUGIVAL

PARIS

LEFT, ASNIÈRES, THE SETTING OF PAINTINGS BY SEURAT
AND OTHER IMPRESSIONIST FOLLOWERS
RIGHT, VÉTHEUIL, MONET'S HOME FROM 1878 TO 1883

INTRODUCTION

The river Seine – especially the stretch between Paris and its mouth at Le Havre – played a special rôle in the development of Impressionism. It provided the artists of the movement with a wealth of motifs. The river itself, its bridges and riverside towns and villages, through the seasons of the year and in its many states from full flood to ice-bound, were infinitely varying themes to which they returned time and time again, as were the fleeting images of sailboats flashing by and fashionable Parisians promenading beside the river or relaxing in riverside restaurants. It was on the Seine that the essential techniques of Impressionism were formulated, and there, through confronting the challenge of depicting on canvas the ephemeral effects of reflections on the water, that its masters were to produce many of their most characteristic and memorable paintings.

Impressionist precursors such as Gustave Courbet (1819-77) had painted the Seine (as in his *Young Women on the Banks of the Seine*, 1857), while Charles-François Daubigny (1817-79) was fascinated by the transient effects of light on water and was probably more influential than any other artist in encouraging the Impressionists to paint this most difficult of subjects (he himself painted from a studio boat on the Oise, an idea later copied by Claude Monet). As Théodore Duret, one of the Impressionists' defenders, explained, 'The Impressionist sits on the bank of a river. The water takes on every possible hue, according to the state of the sky, the perspective, the time of the day, and the calmness or agitation of the air. Without hesitation he paints water which contains every hue.' The Impressionists' 'obsession with water',

MANET'S *CLAUDE MONET IN HIS STUDIO BOAT AT ARGENTEUIL*, 1874

suggested art critic René Huyghe, 'gradually replaced the world of solids .... Earth, trees and sky were to have no further existence of their own but were to become nothing more than fragile reflections, swamped by water, absorbed by it, liquefied into its undulating and vibrant form.' The result, he declared, was 'a vibrato of coloured marks scattering and dancing, dissolving and blending with formerly distinct elements in an atomic waltz of the atmosphere.'

The pervasive influence of the Seine extended beyond the

MONET'S *IMPRESSION: SUNRISE*, PAINTED AT LE HAVRE IN 1872

Impressionists themselves to the writers with whom they were associated. 'I think I loved the Seine as much as I did because it gave me the feeling of being alive,' wrote Guy de Maupassant in his *Mouche, or Reminiscences of a Rowing Man*. In 1885, by which time the Impressionists had become recognized as a significant group, de Maupassant visited their acknowledged leader Claude Monet at Etretat on the Normandy coast. There he observed him at work 'in his search for impressions'. Undertaking his quest, he explained, Monet 'was no longer a painter, in truth, but a hunter . . . . Before his subject the painter lay in wait for the sun and shadows, capturing in a few brush strokes the ray that fell or the cloud that passed.

Etretat lies to the north of Le Havre, and it was there more than twelve years earlier that Monet had produced one of his unique 'impressions' – indeed, naming it *Impression: Sunrise*. This was the painting that was later to provide the Impressionists with their very name. Monet knew Le Havre at the mouth of the Seine well. When he was a five-year-old child, his family had moved to what was already the principal French port serving sea traffic to America. His family was in the grocery business and flourished by supplying provisions to transatlantic ships. Almost inevitably, Claude became interested in boats and drew them from an early age, but he began his artistic career, while still at school, not as a marine artist but as a caricaturist of local personalities. Eugène Boudin (1824-98), a successful local painter, recognized his talent and encouraged Monet to take up landscape painting. Against parental opposition he studied in Paris until he was called up to serve in the army. In 1862, following two years service, he returned to paint with Boudin at Honfleur on the south of the Seine estuary. In the artists' colony that gathered there Monet met the Dutch painter Johan Jongkind (1819-91), from whom he learned new techniques, adopting Jongkind's method of painting the same landscapes at different seasons – a method he was to follow throughout his life, culminating in his major 'series paintings'.

After his resignation from the army, Monet enrolled in the Paris studio of Charles Gleyre (1806-74). In 1864 Gleyre's studio closed and he spent the summer back in Honfleur, painting with Boudin, Jongkind and Frédéric Bazille (1841-70), a fellow student of Gleyre's. The following year, Pierre Auguste Renoir, another of Gleyre's students, wrote to Bazille suggesting he join a group of artists travelling down the Seine by boat from Paris: 'We are going to watch the regattas at Le Havre. We plan to stay about ten days and the entire expense will be about fifty francs. If you wish to come along, this will give me great pleasure. I am taking my paintbox in order to make sketches of any sites I happen to like.' On the trip he was joined by another young painter, Alfred Sisley, the son of an English businessman. In 1865 Monet, now studying in Paris with Courbet, had two marine paintings exhibited at the official art institution, the Salon. They were well received, although, by being hung alphabetically, they ended up next to works by Edouard Manet, with whom Monet – not for the last time – was confused.

Building on his success, in 1866 Monet continued producing

ARTISTS AT WORK IN THE PICTURESQUE HARBOUR AT HONFLEUR

PHOTOGRAPHS OF ALFRED SISLEY (LEFT) AND CAMILLE PISSARRO (RIGHT)

marine subjects in Honfleur, Le Havre and at Sainte-Adresse on the outskirts of Le Havre, developing his technique of painting out of doors and his use of bright colour, which was at the time decidedly unfashionable. The invention of paint in tubes had facilitated open-air oil painting for the first time (oil paint was previously mixed as required for use within a studio, and watercolour was the principal medium used out of doors). Other new techniques were also being introduced, such as the rejection of the use of glazes, particularly among the founders of Impressionism.

At the time of the 1867 Paris World's Fair Monet painted views of the Seine in Paris from high vantage points, in the style of the Japanese prints then becoming popular. Among the subjects he chose was the Pont Neuf, also painted by his friend

GUSTAVE CAILLEBOTTE'S *THE LANDING-STAGE AT ARGENTEUIL*

Renoir, whom he met regularly with fellow artists at their favourite rendezvous, the Café Guerbois.

The year 1868 saw Monet painting at Bennecourt on the Seine, resulting in his *The River*, but it was the following year that was crucial in the development of Impressionism. In 1869 Monet rented a house at Saint-Michel near Bougival. It was an area that was becoming increasingly popular, especially among day-trippers from Paris. Victorien Sardou's *Paris-Guide* of 1867 recommended, 'Set out early in the morning for Bougival, and after a big lunch on the banks of the river, proceed to Marly-le-Roi on the path that goes through Louveciennes.' Renoir, as it happened, was staying with his parents in Louveciennes, a fashionable area on the outskirts of Paris. Between Louveciennes and Bougival on the south bank of the Seine and Chatou on the north, the river divides into two channels. Between them lies Croissy Island (now known as 'Ile

des Impressionistes') adjoining which there was a floating restaurant known as La Grenouillère – a location that has been described as the birthplace of Impressionism. Renoir would have crossed the footbridge at Bougival to reach La Grenouillère where, during the summer of 1869, he worked alongside Monet, producing similar versions of the same subjects and evolving the techniques that were to become the hallmarks of Impressionism, especially the use of comma-like brush-strokes and bright colour. While they worked there they were visited by another founder of Impressionism, Camille Pissarro, who had recently settled in Louveciennes.

In 1870 Monet returned to Le Havre and also worked with Pissarro in Louveciennes, but with the outbreak of the Franco-Prussian War both left for England to avoid being conscripted. It is interesting to note that even in England, Monet found the lure of river scenes irresistible, painting the Thames on numerous occasions during this and subsequent visits – just as he was later to paint watery subjects in Venice. Sisley, being English-born, was not called up, and moved to Voisins where he began painting subjects on the river. Bazille, who had been a major influence through his work and support of his friends, was sadly killed during the War.

In 1871 Monet returned to France and, at the recommendation of Manet, moved into a rented house in Argenteuil on the Seine. Relieved from the horrors of the war and the Commune that followed, France in the 1870s was gripped by a prevailing mood of gaiety and frivolity, not unlike the situation of fifty years later, when the 'roaring twenties' came as an antidote to the gloom of the First World War. Day trips into the countryside became increasingly popular, as did a wide range of outdoor leisure pursuits, among them pleasure boating and sailing. Not long before, Argenteuil had been a rural village, but since the

The attractions of La Grenouillere displayed in a poster for the dance hall and as seen by Monet (top right) and Renoir (bottom right), 1869

building of a rail link to Paris it had been transformed into an increasingly popular and growing industrial town, virtually a suburb of Paris. It was also the closest place to Paris where sailing took place on any scale, and as it had a long straight stretch of river, it became noted for regattas and as the location of the headquarters of the Cercle de la Voile de Paris, the prestigious Paris Sailing Club. At this stage in his career, Monet was permanently short of money and Argenteuil was relatively cheap, but convenient for Paris. It had two bridges, one for road and the other for rail traffic, both of which had been damaged during the war. While they underwent repair, Monet produced paintings of them.

Once again, Monet and Renoir worked together. Renoir also worked on the Seine in Louveciennes and Bougival, and with Sisley who had settled nearby in Marly-le-Roi. Among his many Seine paintings of the period are several of flooding at nearby Port-Marly, executed in 1873, a theme to which he returned in 1876. He also sometimes visited Monet at Argenteuil and painted there.

Monet's Argenteuil period is regarded as the 'golden age' of Impressionism, during which the principal exponents worked in a similar style often described as 'pure Impressionism', typified by the use of bright colour and broken brush strokes. He lived successively in two houses there, the first rented from one of Manet's relatives, later moving to a larger property. Manet, living in Gennevilliers, and Renoir became frequent visitors to Monet's household and painted portraits of each other and their families in the garden. Monet's interest in gardens was developed there and led to a number of paintings on this theme, as well as landscapes of the surrounding countryside. For the first time Manet, previously a committed studio painter, became persuaded that open-air painting offered new possibilities.

MANET'S SUNNY EVOCATION OF THE SEINE IN HIS *ARGENTEUIL*, 1874

VÉTHEUIL FROM THE RIVER, ONE OF MONET'S FAVOURITE VIEWS

Renoir, living in Paris in 1872, painted urban locations, such as the Pont Neuf, but often visited Monet in Argenteuil. For the first time Monet painted something of the industrial landscape, including barges on the river. Occasionally in Impressionist paintings of the period, particularly those of Armand Guillaumin, factory chimneys are glimpsed on the horizon – but most views ignore this evidence of encroaching industrialization in favour of idyllic riverscapes, with man-made elements restricted to boats and bridges. To this extent, the Impressionists may be accused of having idealized their subjects – and certainly few of Monet's paintings of the Seine, such as his *Sunday at Argenteuil*, provide any hint of the bustle of tourism that was already regarded as something of a blight. At Argenteuil in 1872 Monet was joined by Sisley during the summer, and again in 1873. Monet's *Impression: Sunrise* was painted at Le Havre in 1872. In the same year, he painted for the first time at another of the Seine's major cities, Rouen, to which he was to return twenty years later to undertake his great series of paintings of the cathedral. In 1873 he bought a boat and converted it into a floating studio like that of Daubigny.

The year 1874 is significant in the history of Impressionism, for the first Impressionist exhibition was held in April and May, and generally received by visitors and critics alike with bemused bafflement. Among the works shown were Monet's *Impression: Sunrise*. Monet moved house in Argenteuil in the same year and with Renoir spent time with their new-found friend, an amateur painter called Gustave Caillebotte, who was both a sailing enthusiast and sufficiently wealthy to act as a patron of the Impressionists, his large collection of their works being later bequeathed to the French nation.

Monet remained in Argenteuil in 1875 and painted a number of snow scenes, before spending more time in Paris where he worked on his *Gare Saint-Lazare* series, and it was not until 1878 that he resumed his work on the Seine, moving to Vétheuil, downstream from Argenteuil. Sometimes known as Vétheuil-Lavacourt (Vétheuil is on the right bank, Lavacourt

RENOIR'S *THE ROWERS' LUNCH*, PAINTED AT CHATOU IN 1879-80

opposite on the left), it was more rural than his previous residences, with a striking skyline dominated by an imposing twelfth-century church that appears in a number of his subsequent paintings. There he rented a house with the family of Ernest and Alice Hoschedé. Ernest, a Belgian department store owner and businessman, had been a patron of Monet and other painters, but after the failure of his business was compelled to live in relative poverty. As in Argenteuil, Monet, with his extended family, lived successively in two different houses, at opposite ends of the village.

During 1879 Sisley worked at Suresnes while Monet worked on his studio boat at Vétheuil and other locations. He painted landscapes of the village of Vétheuil on numerous occasions and during different seasons, among his most successful being his depictions of the ice floes on the Seine. Renoir, meanwhile, was working at Bougival and Chatou, in particular at the Restaurant Fournaise, resulting in his celebrated *Luncheon of the Boating Party*. Monet left Vétheuil in 1881 (though he was to revisit it twenty years later) and moved briefly to Poissy, on the Seine to the west of Paris, with Alice Hoschedé and their families. Monet's wife Camille had died in 1879. Alice, now separated from Ernest, became Monet's mistress and, following Ernest's death, his wife.

In 1883 Monet settled in Giverny, where he was to remain for the rest of his life, producing further paintings of river scenes on the nearby Seine, the Epte and especially the water-lilies on the lake in his famous garden. 'These landscapes of water and reflections have become an obsession,' he later wrote, and at Giverny and elsewhere he continued to confront the theme of water up to his death in 1926.

By the 1880s the founding fathers of Impressionism had all gone their separate ways. Manet died in 1883 and other members of the group were scattered across France, some, such as Renoir, beginning to question the value and achievements of Impressionism. In 1883 the young Neo-Impressionist Georges Seurat began *The Bathers*, his first major work on the Seine at Asnières in suburban Paris, followed in 1887 with his best-known work, *La Grande Jatte*, also at Asnières, a location to which other Impressionist followers including van Gogh were drawn. Post-Impressionists such as Maximilien Luce at Herblay and Signac at Les Andelys maintained the Impressionists' fascination with the Seine. Their successors, especially the Fauves Maurice de Vlaminck (1876-1958) and André Derain (1880-1954), returned to Chatou, and Raoul Dufy (1877-1953) to Le Havre, continuing the intimate relationship of painters and the Seine well into the twentieth century.

THE PLATES

JOHN SINGER SARGENT, *PAUL HELLEU SKETCHING WITH HIS WIFE*, 1889

Monet's first major Impressionist painting executed on the Seine shows his mistress Camille Doncieux, whom he was to marry in 1870, seated on the river bank, their rowing boat moored below. At the time, they were living in Bennecourt at the recommendation of the writer Emile Zola, who knew it from his previous visits to his friend Paul Cézanne, a former resident. Zola visited them there and later featured an artist and his companion's visit to Bennecourt and their exploration of the river in his novel, *L'Oeuvre*. Monet was living in dire poverty at the time and was eventually ejected from the inn where he, Camille and their son Jean were staying. In the depths of despair, he attempted to commit suicide.

La Grenouillère (literally, 'the frog pond') was a restaurant connected to Croissy Island, near Bougival, to the west of Paris. In the 1860s it became a popular spot for Parisian day-trippers, offering picnicking, boating and bathing and lively entertainment. According to de Maupassant it was a venue for 'journalists, show-offs, young men with private incomes, scoundrels, degenerates and rogues'. Monet and Renoir painted there together during the summer of 1869, but on 25 September Monet wrote to Bazille, 'Here I've come to a standstill, from lack of paints! I alone this year will have done nothing. It makes me rage against everyone . . . I have a dream, a picture of bathing at La Grenouillère, for which I've made some bad sketches, but it's a dream. Renoir, who has been spending two months here, also wants to do this picture.' In this, the finished version of his 'dream' painting, he looks downstream from the restaurant, toward the village of Rueil, with the bathers arranged on the gangplank leading to the floating restaurant and splashing in the water beyond. Renoir painted a very similar subject at the same time. Monet's *La Grenouillère* is regarded as fusion of all his experimental work, especially his representation of the effects of light on the water and use of bright colour in a single masterpiece.

In 1867 Renoir had painted the Pont des Arts and other views of urban Paris along the Seine, as had Monet in the same year. Renoir's *Pont Neuf* indicates the influence of photography – it is almost a 'snapshot' of the bridge with the bustle of traffic, pedestrians and traders. He arrested their motion by sending his brother Edmond onto the bridge to stop passers-by with such ruses as asking them for the time, whereupon Renoir, seated outside a café at the corner of the quai du Louvre, sketched them. The Pont Neuf is the oldest bridge in Paris and straddles two arms of the Seine, linking La Cité with each bank, and we see the statue of King Henri IV to the right, with a bathing establishment below the bridge and the buildings on the quai de l'Horloge on the left which have altered little since Renoir's day. Pissarro also painted the Pont Neuf, and Monet painted precisely the same view the following year, but in the rain and in a very sketchy style. One of the major differences between Renoir and Monet also comes out in their two versions of the same subject. Renoir is clearly more interested in people and their interaction, Monet in landscapes in which people are almost an incidental component.

In 1875, before the Impressionists became highly regarded, this painting was sold for 300 Francs. At the time of Renoir's death in 1919 it was sold again for 100,000 Francs – a measure of the reversal from rejection to acceptance of Impressionism within the lifetimes of some of its exponents.

'The animation of the canvas is one of the hardest problems of painting. To give life to the work of art is certainly one of the most necessary tasks of the true artist. Everything must serve this end: form, colour, surface. The artist's impression is the life-giving factor, and only this impression can free that of the spectator.'

Alfred Sisley, Letter to Adolphe Tavernier, January 1872

Sisley produced several paintings of the village of Villeneuve-la-Garenne, to the east of Argenteuil, some of them showing the bridge, as well as several of the banks of the Seine near Bougival, with trees similarly intersecting the canvas. The work was bought in 1872 for 350 francs by Paul Durand-Ruel (1831-1922), the dealer who did most to help the Impressionists. He in turn sold it in 1898 to the Russian collector Serge Stchoukine, and it later found its way into the Hermitage collection.

ARMAND GUILLAUMIN (1841–1927)
SEINE QUAI NEAR PARIS, 1873
Private collection

In 1868 Guillaumin, an employee of the Paris railway, relinquished his job to devote the rest of his life to painting. Although he worked closely with such artists as Pissarro, and produced many highly accomplished works, he never achieved the success of his fellow Impressionists. However, as the result of a substantial lottery win, he had the financial resources to enable him to work untroubled by the financial difficulties that plagued other members of the movement. A contemporary critic described Guillaumin's paintings as displaying 'the confidence of a genuine emotion confronting nature', and his depictions of the Seine in different seasons, often featuring sunrises and sunsets, are among his most striking works. In a series of pictures executed at Ivry and Paris, he often focussed on the Seine, but unlike the other Impressionists, he was not averse to showing its industrial aspect, crowded with coal barges and flanked by commercial buildings. His *Sunset at Ivry* (1873), for example, is a depiction of the Seine with belching factory chimneys.

EDOUARD MANET (1832-83)
BOATING, 1874
Metropolitan Museum of Art, New York; Bequest of Mrs H.O. Havemeyer, 1929
The Havemeyer Collection

The writer J-K Huysmans visited the Salon and saw *Boating* on display. It had caused a furore, but, he reported, 'His other canvas, *Boating*, is just as unusual [as Manet's *The Conservatory*]. The bright blue water continues to exasperate a number of people. Water isn't that colour? I beg your pardon, it is, at certain times, just as it has green and grey times, just as it contains lavender, and slate-grey, and light-buff reflections at other times. One must make up one's own mind to look about. And there lies one of the great errors of contemporary landscape painters who, coming upon a river with a preconceived formula, do not establish between it, the sky reflected in it, the position of the banks which border it, the time and season as they are at the moment they are painting, the necessary accord which nature always establishes. Manet has never, thank heavens, known those prejudices stupidly maintained in the academies. He paints, by abbreviations, nature as it is and as he sees it.'

PIERRE AUGUSTE RENOIR (1841-1919)
THE SEINE AT ARGENTEUIL, 1874
The Portland Art Museum; Bequest of Winslow B. Ayer

Sailing and rowing were among the most popular leisure activities of middle-class Parisians in the 1870s, and Argenteuil was the most fashionable location for pleasure-boating and regattas. *The Seine at Argenteuil* was painted from the Petit-Gennevilliers side of the river, near the Pont d'Argenteuil – one arch of the bridge and the toll house can be seen on the far right. Having worked alongside Monet at La Grenouillère in 1869, Renoir repeatedly stayed with the Monet family in subsequent years. The use of fragmented brush strokes seen in this work is more typical of Monet than Renoir during this period, and indicates the strength of Monet's influence. There is a work by Monet from the same period that is almost identical, except that the man seen on the slipway has climbed into the boat.

CLAUDE MONET (1840-1926)
ARGENTEUIL (RED BOATS), 1875
Musée d'Orsay, Paris

'Claude Monet loves water, and it is his special gift to portray its mobility and transparency, be it sea or river, grey and monotonous, or coloured by the sky. I have never seen a boat posed more lightly on the water than in his pictures, or a veil more mobile and light than his moving atmosphere. It is in truth a marvel.'

Stéphane Mallarmé, *Art Monthly Review*, September 1876

In one of several paintings executed from the same vantage point depicting the clinker-built boat on the right and the red sailing dinghies behind, Monet depicts a scene of the river undisturbed by people. His image of the tranquillity of a summer's day in Argenteuil is perhaps somewhat romanticized, since by the 1870s Argenteuil had become overrun with Parisians at weekends as their enthusiasm for outdoor life gained momentum.

PAUL GAUGUIN (1848-1903)
THE SEINE AT THE PONT D'IENA 1875
Musée d'Orsay, Paris

Paul Gauguin, a latecomer to the Impressionist circle, produced few urban paintings. His *Seine at the Pont d'Iéna*, a subject that attracted other Impressionists, including Berthe Morisot, was executed in 1875, early in his career and soon after he met and fell under the influence of Pissarro. Gauguin was a godson of Gustave Arosa, one of Pissarro's patrons and a collector of Impressionist paintings, and through this connection met Pissarro and took lessons from him. At the time, Gauguin was working as a successful banker and avidly collected works by such artists as Sisley and Pissarro before relinquishing his business activities to devote his life to painting, impoverishing himself and his family as a result.

ALFRED SISLEY (1839-99)
THE FLOOD AT PORT-MARLY, 1876
Musée d'Orsay, Paris

'Sisley is a great and beautiful artist; in my opinion, he is a master equal to the greatest. I have seen works of his of rare amplitude and beauty, among others a *Flood* which is a masterpiece.'

Camille Pissarro

One of Sisley's great and typically unpretentious works, it is similar to a painting he had produced in 1872. With the repeat of widespread flooding in 1876 he returned enthusiastically to the theme. It was one of four paintings of the same view, which he executed along with others showing different aspects of the flood that affected Port-Marly. Like Monet, Sisley revelled in painting threateningly storm-laden skies and the effects of light on water. In his lifetime Sisley achieved little success. After being exhibited at the third Impressionist exhibition in 1876, *The Flood at Port-Marly* was sold for just 180 francs. In 1900, the year after his death, it changed hands for 43,000 francs, and was bequeathed to the Louvre in 1908.

ALFRED SISLEY (1839-99)
THE SEINE AT SURESNES, 1877
Musée d'Orsay, Paris

'He became the painter of rivers that sparkled with spangles and lights, and beautiful light and deep skies in which the pink of the morning, the blue of the day and the violet of evening melt away and the clouds sail on in the flowing ether like squadrons.'

Gustave Geffroy, *La Vie Artistique*, 1897

Sisley's painting shows a stretch of the Seine with the bridge at Suresnes, in what is now a built-up suburb of Paris, in the background. The Impressionist technique is here employed to the full to convey the suggestion of the wind rippling the water, causing the grass to quiver and the clouds to streak by. It was painted at the time of Sisley's direst poverty – in 1878 he offered Duret no fewer than 30 paintings in return for 500 francs a month for six months. However, it was acquired by Gustave Caillebotte and as part of his collection was bequeathed to the French nation.

PIERRE AUGUSTE RENOIR (1841-1919)
OARSMEN AT CHATOU, 1879
National Gallery of Art, Washington DC; Gift of Samuel A. Lewisohn

After spending part of the summer of 1879 on the coast at Berneval, Renoir went to Chatou where he painted this work, his first to feature Aline Charigot, a dressmaker and the laundress to both Renoir and Monet when they lived in Paris, who was later seen in his *Luncheon of the Boating Party* and eventually became Renoir's wife. The Impressionists' patron, painter and boating enthusiast Gustave Caillebotte, who also appears in *Luncheon of the Boating Party*, here stands in the foreground. The figures are noticeably less impressionistic than the background, which is typical of Renoir's evolving style in this period.

Although known by the alternative title of *The Seine at Asnières*, the location of later works by Seurat, van Gogh and other followers of the Impressionists, it is by no means certain that it was actually painted there. Renoir creates a striking contrast between the bright blue water and the orange boat in a painting that has affinities with paintings by Monet – the train on the bridge on the right is reminiscent of Monet's paintings of the rail bridge at Argenteuil – and in some respects it is a precursor of Monet's paintings of girls in boats painted at Giverny in 1887-90. The work was once owned by Victor Chocquet (1821-1891), one of the Impressionists' patrons.

Berthe Morisot lived at Bougival at intervals from 1881 to 1884 and frequently painted landscapes along the Seine. This work, however, was probably painted in Paris on the lake in the Bois de Boulogne which lies between two arms of the Seine. Morisot was the only woman whose works were exhibited in the first Impressionist exhibition, and, except for the year 1879, when this work was painted and when her daughter Julie was born, showed at all exhibitions from 1874 to 1886. Married to Manet's brother, she had continual contact with and was a significant member of the Impressionist group, but as a result of the social constraints of the day, her sex and rank prescribed the subject matter of her paintings, so that images of women and children in domestic settings predominate in her oeuvre. As Paul Valéry explained, 'Her paintings taken all together remind one of what a woman's diary would be like if she expressed herself in colour and design instead of in writing.'

At Vétheuil, where his wife Camille had died the previous September, Monet tried to detach himself from his misery by painting out of doors in one of the worst winters in memory, during which the town was cut off from the outside world. Alice, the wife of Ernest Hoschedé, a former patron of Monet's, and their six children were all living with Monet at the time. As the the ice broke up she wrote to her husband, telling him, 'At five in the morning, I was woken up by a frightful noise, like the rumbling of thunder . . . on top of this frightening noise came cries from Lavacourt; very quickly I was at the windows and despite considerable obscurity saw white masses hurtling about; this time it was the debacle, the real thing.' Monet's paintings of the resultant ice floes on the river, described by J-K Huysmans as 'intensely melancholy', have been seen as anticipating his famous water-lily pictures executed at Giverny. Monet returned to the theme of ice floes on the river in the winter of 1892-93.

Pierre Auguste Renoir (1841-1919)
Luncheon of the Boating Party, 1880-81
Phillips Collection, Washington DC

'It was a perpetual party. I was always satiated at Fournaises. I found all the superb girls that I could desire. My friends knew that, for me, a woman is only a pretext for a picture.'

Pierre Auguste Renoir

'The Impressionists show their particular talent and attain the summit of their art when they paint our French Sundays . . . kisses in the sun, picnics, complete rest, not a thought about work, unashamed relaxation.'

René Gimpel

Started in summer 1880, but finished in his studio early in 1881, *Luncheon of the Boating Party* shows an upstairs terrace at the Restaurant Fournaise at Chatou, looking downstream toward Chatou railway bridge. It is effectively a riverside version of Renoir's previously most ambitious painting, *Ball at the Moulin de la Galette* (1876) which similarly shows Parisians at play and flirting lovers. The identity of the subjects in this 'capital study of French faces and forms', as a critic in the *New York Times* described it in 1886, has been the subject of much argument since it was painted. It seems certain it features a number of Renoir's close friends, among whom the girl on the left holding a dog is Aline Charigot, who later married Renoir. Alphonse Fournaise, the son of the restaurant's owner, is leaning on the rail, while on the right Gustave Caillebotte – who once owned Renoir's *Moulin de la Galette* – sits astride a chair.

'We were at Lavacourt, a little town opposite Vétheuil. The light was soft and serene, and the last, broad rays of the sun were spreading over the village, spangling the silk of the Seine with its lights and fending off the shadows that were lightly blurring the tree-tops and enveloping the foliage with darkening green.'

Emile Taboureux, *La Vie Moderne*, 1880

In the years 1878-81, Monet painted many views of Vétheuil dominated by its distinctive church. Seeing them exhibited, J-K Huysmans noted, 'How his rivers flow, speckled by the teeming colours of things they reflect; how the light, cold gusts rise from the water in his paintings, into the leaves and through the blades of the grass!'

'Under a blazing mid-afternoon summer sky, we see the Seine flooded with sunshine, smart town houses on the opposite bank, and small steamboats, sail-boats and a skiff moving up and down the river.' So began Jules Christophe's description of the painting in *Men of Today* (1890), not long after Seurat's most famous work had been received with hostility at the eighth and last Impressionist exhibition. The setting for this remarkable subject is the public park on the island of La Grande Jatte, not far from Asnières, also the location of Seurat's painting, *The Bathers* (1883-84). Visiting the island during the morning over a period of several months, Seurat made frequent sketches and studies – some completely devoid of the promenading Parisians who inhabit the finished work – progressively assembling the innumerable elements of the painting. He then returned to his studio in the afternoons to work on the final composition, into which he also incorporated portions drawn from fashion plates and caricatures. Its wealth of detail and meticulous pointillist technique still have the power to convey the impact it caused when originally shown.

The Parisian suburb of Courbevoie attracted a number of the Impressionists and their followers, among them the young Vincent van Gogh. Seurat's representation of the bridge introduces an unusual series of verticals, comprising masts, factory chimneys and people, crossed by the horizontal bridge and landing-stage. Its very static and ordered impression of the Seine is radically different from the life and movement conveyed by the previous generation of painters, such as Monet, and marks a new direction in the scientifically-based art of the New-Impressionists.

Signac was a devoted follower of the Impressionists. Although he never had any formal art training, he came under the influence of Seurat in 1884, and was close to Pissarro and van Gogh. He adopted the technique of pointillism in 1886 and applied it predominantly in his work as a landscape painter. He was on close terms with Caillebotte, with whom he shared an interest in sailing, and his subjects consequently often included Seine locations. In summer 1886 he painted at Les Andelys, a village between Vernon and Rouen, and also at Asnières, Herblay, Sannois and the Ile de la Cité in Paris. At the end of the nineteenth century, Signac was visited in the South of France by Matisse and Derain, founders of the Fauve movement, in whose work the Impressionist legacy was carried into the present century

CLAUDE MONET (1840-1926)
THE BOAT AT GIVERNY, 1887
Musée d'Orsay, Paris

'Water takes pride of place in Monet's work. He is the painter of water *par excellence*. In older landscape paintings, water looks motionless and monotonous with its "water" colour, like a simple mirror to reflect objects. In Monet's paintings, water no longer has its own unvaried colour. It takes on an infinite variety of appearances according to the condition of the atmosphere, the type of bed over which it flows, or the silt that it carries along. It can be clear, opaque, calm, agitated, fast-flowing or sleepy, depending on the temporary conditions observed by the artist as he sets his easel before its liquid surface.'

Théodore Duret, *The Impressionist Painters*, 1878

Monet spoke of the challenge of painting that which it is 'impossible to do', including in this category the grass that grows on the river bed and can be seen, through the reflections, flowing in the current. This he achieved in many of his works undertaken at his final home at Giverny, just off the Seine, on the Epte tributary to the west of Vétheuil, where he settled with Alice Hoschedé whom he later married. Their combined families were large and their children grew up on the river, spending happy days in their boat the *Norvégienne*, or *Norwegian*, described by Monet's stepson Jean-Pierre Hoschedé as 'a light boat with a round deck floor'. After repeatedly losing it when it was cut adrift on the Seine, Monet bought a stretch of river frontage so that he was able to moor it safely.

A full-time soldier and self-taught amateur painter, Dubois-Pillet worked in Paris in the 1880s, when he was posted to Le Puy, where he died. Despite his rank as a Commander in Republican Guard, he maintained a bohemian lifestyle and circle of friends that was at odds with his career, as were his left-wing political leanings. Dubois-Pillet was responsible in 1884 for conceiving the idea of the Société des Artistes Indépendants, an organization devoted to exhibiting the works of revolutionary artists. In doing so, according to Signac, 'He brings together the isolated, the misunderstood, the despised. He fashions a dazzling display of Seurat, Signac, himself and the new adepts.' With his close friends Signac and Seurat, Dubois-Pillet developed the technique of pointillism to a highly complex degree, based as much in the science of optics as in the traditions of painting.

A wealthy amateur artist, Caillebotte was a highly talented painter whose reputation has been eclipsed by the more famous Impressionists such as his friends Monet and Renoir, with whom he showed at their exhibitions. He acquired a house in Petit-Gennevilliers, next to Argenteuil, in about 1882, at first dividing his time alternately with his residence in the Boulevard Haussmann, Paris, and permanently from 1897 until his death seven years later at the age of 45. He produced a number of paintings of the Seine and its tributaries during this period, and owing to his particular interest in racing yachts, works showing sailing boats at Argenteuil feature strongly in his oeuvre. His masterful execution of reflections of light on water and subtle changes of light have been compared with those of Monet. His *Banks of the Seine at Argenteuil* was exhibited publicly only once, in 1894, shortly after his death, and remained in private hands until it was sold in 1990.

MAXIMILIEN LUCE (1858-1941)
THE SEINE AT HERBLAY, 1890
Musée d'Orsay, Paris

'Applied talent, patient study, a taste for large beautiful forms enveloped in atmosphere.'

Gustave Geoffroy

After starting his artistic career as a wood engraver, Maximilien Luce turned to painting in the 1880s, studying under the society painter Carolus-Duran (1838-1917) before coming under the influence of Seurat and Pissarro at the time when the latter was passing through a pointillist phase. He executed a number of landscapes in his distinctive style in and around Paris, including this work at Herblay, which lies on the Seine to the north-west of Argenteuil. The following year, Luce's work was represented in the first Symbolist exhibition.

CAMILLE PISSARRO (1830-1903)
THE PILOT'S JETTY, LE HAVRE, 1903
Tate Gallery, London

Paintings of Seine scenes are not prominent in Pissarro's output. He lived in Pontoise for many years and gravitated towards the river Oise, although he occasionally painted on the Seine at such locations as Marly and Rouen and, like Renoir, Monet and others of the Impressionist circle, the Pont-Neuf in Paris. Pissarro fell under the spell of Seurat and the Neo-Impressionists and adopted their pointillist style for several years before renouncing the method and the limitations it imposed, although elements of its influence persisted when he returned to his former Impressionist technique. Pissarro's *The Pilot's Jetty, Le Havre* was painted in the year of his death and exemplifies the continuity of Impressionism and the allure of the Seine well into the twentieth century.

Published in the United States of America
in 1992
by UNIVERSE
300 Park Avenue South
New York, NY 10010

ISBN 0-87663-620-2

92 93 94 95/10 9 8 7 6 5 4 3 2 1

Produced, edited and designed by Russell Ash & Bernard Higton

Printed in Spain

Library of Congress Cataloging-in-Publication Data

The Impressionists' river: views of the Seine.
p. cm.
ISBN 0-87663-620-2
1. Impressionism (Art)—France.   2. Painting, French.
3. Painting, Modern—19th century—France.   4. Seine River (France)
in art.
ND547.5.I415   1991
759.4′09′034—dc20   91-26383   CIP

Picture credits
All plates are from the sources shown in the captions unless
otherwise indicated below.
Additional picture sources: Front cover (Pierre Auguste
Renoir, *The Skiff,* c.1879) National Gallery, London;
1 (Gustave Caillebotte, *Sailboats at Argenteuil,* c.1888),
2 (Claude Monet, *Sunday at Argenteuil,* 1872) Musée d'Orsay,
Paris/Bridgeman Art Library; 4 Map of the Impressionists'
Seine by David Atkinson, photos © Cap-Viollet; 5 Neue
Pinakothek, Munich; 6 Musée Marmottan, Paris, photo
Lauros Giraudon; 7 left, centre 21, 31, 35 Photographie
Giraudon; 7 right, 11 © Cap-Viollet; 8 Private collection/
Photographie Giraudon; 9 left Roger-Viollet; 9 top right
(Claude Monet, *La Grenouillère,* 1869) The Metropolitan
Museum of Art, Bequest of Mrs H. O. Havemeyer, 1929. The
H. O. Havemeyer Collection; 9 bottom right (Pierre Auguste
Renoir, *La Grenouillère,* 1869) Oskar Reinhart Foundation,
Winterthur; 10 Musée des Beaux-Arts, Tournai/Photographie
Giraudon; 12 The Art Institute of Chicago, Potter Palmer
Collection; 13 Brooklyn Museum, New York/Bridgeman Art
Library; 23, 59 © Christie's; 29, 57, Back cover (Claude
Monet, *Argenteuil (Red Boats),* 1875) Bridgeman Art Library/
Photographie Giraudon; 33, 55 © Photo RMN; 43, 45, 47,
49, 53, 61, 63 Bridgeman Art Library.